God with us!
God is good!
Blessings to you
and yours.

Audrey Marie

They Call Him Immanuel, God With Us

They Call Him Immanuel, God With Us

✦

A Christian Poetry Devotional for Inspiration and Reflection

Poetry and photography from the hand and heart of Audrey Marie

iUniverse, Inc.

New York Lincoln Shanghai

They Call Him Immanuel, God With Us
A Christian Poetry Devotional for Inspiration and Reflection

iUniverse, Inc.

For information address:
iUniverse, Inc.
2021 Pine Lake Road, Suite 100
Lincoln, NE 68512
www.iuniverse.com

All poetry and photographs are exclusively the author's.
All references to the Bible are from the King James version.

ISBN: 0-595-29498-7 (pbk)
ISBN: 0-595-66010-X (cloth)

Printed in the United States of America

To Grandma Rosie,
who taught and inspired me and others
to love God and to love and write poetry.

And to my husband, for his love and support,
and to all of my family, friends and students
who are dear to me and inspired many of these poems.

And with thanks to God,
who is
the greatest source of all inspiration.

Contents

Acknowledgments

As a young child my Grandmother Rosie taught me to love and write poetry. She herself was a published poet. For a while, she wrote a newspaper column featuring poetry, and she also had a radio program for reading poetry. However, what really stayed with me were not her accomplishments, but the love she had in her heart for the beauty of poetry, her love for me and my family, and her love for God. She had me keep books of my poetry when I was a child. Due to changes in my life, those books were lost. But the lessons of them were not. Two of the poems in this book, at the core, are from those very early writing times: *Tick Tock* and *Never Give Up*. I remembered how I originally wrote each poem in my childhood poetry book, and then as an adult I updated them. Grandma Rosie has resided for a long time now with the great "author and finisher of our faith," but her loving inspiration and influence continues with me and in this book.

Often there is a particular person or a very specific moment that is the inspiration for a poem. Many of these poems I clearly can connect in my mind to a specific person or persons who were the catalyst for the poem. *Fifty Wishes* was written for my brother, Charles, who is also a poet. *I Wish* was inspired by numerous family members and friends who are now with the Lord, when I found myself saying when I thought of each of them: "I wish…" I thought of my mother, my younger brother, John, and my grandparents, Rosie, Gracie and Charlie, my stepsister Sherry, and old family friends Lill, Warren, Lou, and a dear friend, Rita. *I Wish* was first published in the Christian Liberty Academy magazine, *Bias*, when I chose to publish it in a memorial issue that was dedicated to the Reverend Paul Lindstrom.

The seed for this book was planted, or maybe more clearly watered, by the poem *And So We Say Goodbye*. This poem was written for my student, Andy, and his parents, Rita and Werner Domitro, who left us "too soon from our tiny, tiny point of view."

We Love Our Soldiers was written in response to a woman I do not know, a mother who wanted to keep front and center in the minds of Americans that our men and women, our soldiers, are still defending freedom overseas.

A Fireman's Daughter was written as a gift for my father, Charles, a retired firefighter, and *My Mom Said* was written in memory of my mother, Kathleen, or Kitty. I have had for many years a very sweet second mom, Barbara. *When Grandma Put Her China Out* was written remembering the special celebration times at Grandma and Grandpa's, Gracie and Charlie's home.

If God was written as a thank you gift for the Dau family, especially Jim and Peggy. They now work for The Voice of the Martyrs ministry. Peggy once said, "If you could clean this room, you could live here." I cleaned the room and stayed over two years in their home. A friend, Jean Cole-Michalec, was also invited to live in the Dau home and was part of the shared "smiles, laughter and tears…loving arms and listening ears."

I am grateful to my husband, Ross, for his love and support. I have written a poem about my husband and me, but it is not in this book. However, his support is clearly part of the weaving of the fabric of this poetry devotional. Also the love and support of many other family members is part of that precious fabric. I am grateful for the love of Lauren, Christopher and David as the children of my heart. I have also been blessed with many wonderful friends in my life. Deborah Wolfe helped me bring this book to completion. Deborah Wilhoite and Shirley Drazba also were used by God to inspire me in this endeavor. I have had many friends show me *Friendship Through the Fire*; special among them since the earliest years of my life is Jeanne Davito-Reilly.

I am also grateful for the inspiration I have received from my many students through the years. *Goodbye, Hello* was inspired by a conversation I had with a student, Elizabeth Guerrero, upon graduation. *Guts and a Heart* was in process, but then was influenced by hearing that a former student, Jeff Aiello, was going to become a police officer.

There are more nuances and influences that I could include about the meaning and inspiration for each poem; but I will conclude that I am so grateful that the greatest source of all inspiration is my Heavenly Father, and I am his loved child. *"For in Him we live, and move, and have our being;* ***as certain also of your own poets have said,*** *For we are also his offspring. "*—Acts 17:28

Poems, Dreams and Butterflies

A poem is like a butterfly flutter of the wing,
A very quick, oh so quick, and beautiful thing.
Catch a glimpse. Words alight,
Then take flight,
Land upon the heart.
Leaving only a sweet memory, they quickly depart.

Poems, dreams and butterflies
Disappear from view,
But those that touch upon the heart still flutter deep inside of you.

A dream is like a butterfly flutter of the wing,
A very fragile, oh so fragile, and beautiful thing.
Dreams begin small in the starry night.
Disappearing from our sight
In the glaring light of day,
Their fragile beauty vanishes. They fly away.

Poems, dreams and butterflies
Take time to reach their grandest form.
They metamorphose; they transform.

The first stage is the smallest; inspiration begins to develop.
Stage two, the change is to a caterpillar that then must envelop
Itself in darkness in the cocoon of change; it must be left to grow.

This is the bleakest stage, the darkest passage to go.
Don't give up now; now would be too soon.
A poem, a dream, a butterfly
Will in time, break forth from its cocoon.

Poems, dreams and butterflies
Need wings to take flight.
Wings do not develop overnight.

Poems, dreams and butterflies
Each need a creator.
God created butterflies,
But poems and dreams are a gift from our Maker
For us to breathe life into and let them metamorphose.
Then like butterflies,
Our poems, our dreams, will become something glorious.

◆   ◆   ◆

In the beginning God created…

So God created
man in his own image, in the image of God
created he him; male and female
created he them

Genesis 1:1a and 1:27

◆   ◆   ◆

We are made in the Creator's image, and we are creators, too. God allowed time to be an ingredient in his creation. It was not until the seventh day that God said that he was finished with the work of his creation. Allow time for that which you dream about, desire or create and work toward, to reach its fulfillment. And hold on during the humble times. Zechariah 7:10 says: *Who has despised the days of small things?* The inspirations stage is beautiful; but the caterpillar stage is homely and the cocoon is dark. The glorious butterfly comes after all of these stages. So, do not stop too soon. Job 8:7 states: *"Though thy beginning was small, yet thy latter end shall greatly increase."*

Remember even if you've stopped listening to a dream, or it seems to have flown away in the glaring light of day, that which is deeply meaningful, that you have dreamed of creating, doing, or that you have hoped to see come to pass, it still flutters within your heart. So start listening to the flutter in your heart, and be willing to let your dreams metamorphose and reach fullness. The Psalmist said, *Delight yourself in God,* who has created you to be a creator, too. God is the one who caused the "flutter" in your heart of that dream, that goal, or deep desire; and he will fulfill it.

But do your part, and do not stop before completion.

God gives us the desires of our hearts.

In the beginning God created…

Tick Tock

It may be very short and yet, it may be far too long.
It may set a destiny, heal a wound, or retell a heart broke song.
But the heartbreak that it brought, it can take away.
It carries with it the darkest night, but also
the dawn of a beautiful, new day.
It makes the sands of the hourglass slip down,
And in the world, it's everywhere to be found.
But it's different if you're in North America on the coast of Maine;
It's different than on the continent of Europe
along the shores of Spain.
And even though it changes, it remains the same here or there.
You can't go back or forward to it; you're only in
that moment of it anywhere.
You can't leave it beneath you, if you climb the highest peak.
You can't lose it in the deepest ocean, if that's what you seek.
It's walking with you, in front of you; it's right behind you, too.
It chases you and races you; it's always there,
but never will it wait for you.
And even though for you or any person, it won't wait,
Because of it you will wait and wait; and it
can make you early or too late.
It seems so quick when you're busy
and when you're having fun; this is true.
But it's so slow when you're sorrowful and blue,

or when there's nothing to do.
It fools us, cajoles us, mocks us and makes a liar of us, too.
We say we don't have it, but ah ha! We always do.
Refer to it by hours or simply minutes;
Every day we all get the same allotment.
No matter if you call it seconds, each day,
we all have the same amount of it.
We need it when we dance, sing or speak,
and to tell a joke right.
Because of it we say, it's begun or over,
good morning and good night.
We give it to others, but it's something we don't own or store.
Some say it's funny; some say it's money,
and some want much more.
Because we sometimes think there's just not enough.
But those who know it well will call your bluff.
It's infinite, eternal, a never ever-ending thing,
But wearing a disguise, it seems to end
when you hear the bell ring.
It can be your friend or a fierce competitor, a foe.
But in the end—though there is no end—we know,
Whether it's your friend or foe, it's for you to decide.
But no matter your choice, from it you cannot hide.
People say it moves like a slow shuffling old snail.
People say it flies furiously fast, across years it will sail.
Every new year people say it looks like a fatherly old man
With a white beard, carrying a baby in his hand.
It steadily moves its hands, and it swiftly moves our feet,
We look at its face, but it's not a person that we meet.

It holds some people prisoner, but it's a choice they make.
Others realize that's erroneous, an error, a serious mistake.
Tick tock, tick tock, tick tock, turn the clock, it will do.
Almost time to end this rhyme—for it is time. Will it capture you?
Or will you be free of its demands? One, two,
three, four, five, six, seven,
A time for every purpose under Heaven.
Eight, nine, ten, and eleven, twelve midnight and noon, it's quick.
And it's slow. And around and around the clock again it goes—tick
tock, tick.

◆   ◆   ◆

He hath made everything beautiful in his time…
God shall judge the righteous and the wicked: for there is a time there for
every purpose and for every work. Ecclesiates 3:11a,17

◆   ◆   ◆

The enigma we call time, as said in the poem, "It…makes a liar of
us…We say we don't have it, but ah ha! We always do."
Remember, "*there is a time for every purpose under Heaven.*" For every-
thing that is important for us to do, there is enough time.

He hath made everything beautiful in his time

Fifty Wishes

Fifty is a good number,
so here's fifty wishes wished for you.
And here's the first wish:
May they all come true.
The next and most important, may you know God's love.
We'll start from the top and work down from above.
May you know God's there for you and know God cares,
And may you find time to kneel each day
and trust God with your prayers.

May you find joy in your family,
even when there's pain.
May you remember the wisdom:
flowers only grow where there's rain.
Regardless of their faults, since you have them too,
May you always be grateful for the parents God gave you.
And when you count your blessings,
may you count your siblings, too,
Or may there be friends who are like a brother or sister to you.
And may you find a soul mate before your life is through.

May you make a difference
in the life of a child you know.
May there be children in your life
that you love and help grow,

And may those children grow up to bring
happiness back your way,
And may you always have someone to say I love you to
at the end of the day.

May you have extended family and friends
who will share your path of life.
These are often the people who will see you through life's strife.
May you be content with your acquaintances,
people who come and go,
But may there be silver and some golden friends you truly know.

May you have time to play, work that brings you satisfaction
and even money,
And when you have difficult times,
may you still find life funny.
May you find reward in the things you set out to do.
And if at first you don't succeed,
may you have the will to try again, too.
May you have the faith to go on when there is a closed door.
May you never be too rich and never too poor.

That you would always see the preciousness of life,
things both great and small.
May you truly find the balance to appreciate it all.
May you find wealth inside of you, and who you are, treasure.
And may you share the same with others,
and give without measure.

May you find hope in the darkness,
and always share the light.

May you have the strength to keep on going
in a worthy battle or a fight,
But may you know when to surrender when
it's the honest thing to do.
And may honesty be a trait you're known for.
May you always be called true.

May your greatest accomplishments
be a blessing to all.
And may you never be too big
that you wouldn't do something small.
May you take responsibility, and know when you're not to blame,
May you still remain humble, even when receiving acclaim.

May you have your share of happiness
and not lose heart when life seems sad.
May the times you made the hard choices, later make you glad.
May you see the value of your life, exactly where and who you are,
And may you share that with others, those both near and far.
May you be sorry when you're wrong, forgiven and forgiving.
May you live a life of giving; may you live a life worth living.

May you go on when necessary,
and may you know when to let go, too.
And when it's time to let go of this life,
may you be satisfied with you.
May you know you finished the job God placed you here to do.
And now we're back to the beginning,
wishing for you—
fifty wishes. May they all come true.

◆   ◆   ◆

I know the plans I have for you
saith the Lord,
plans to prosper you
and not to harm you,
plans to give you a hope and a future.
Jeremiah 29:11

◆   ◆   ◆

What the Lord said
contains more than fifty wishes. It encompasses the seed of everything
good for God's children—prosperity, protection, *a hope and a future*
planned by God. God's plan is more sublime and infinitely vaster for
us than the exact fulfillment of fifty wishes. The *hope*, the *future* which
God has for us with Him is so very much larger; it includes here and
now on earth, and into eternity. Fifty wishes could not begin to
encompass the grander plan of God for His children; fifty wishes is
truly small. But for each of us in our small way, doing our part in and
for God's eternal kingdom, it's still a nice place to start:
wishing for others—fifty wishes.

I know the plans I have for you, saith the Lord...
plans to give you a hope and a future

Every Wish

Every wish
is really a prayer,
A longing in the heart hidden there,
A hoping someone answers from somewhere.
Every wish is really a soul's prayer.

Wishes
can make us happy or sad.
Choose carefully the words you wish when mad.
Words we choose make us sorrowful or glad.
Choose wisely. Wishes can be good or bad.

Wishes
can vary in type and size,
Some granted by surprise to young, or old and wise.
A special gift that was desired by our longing eyes
Is often given to us with the word shouted, surprise!

Wishes
can be often very, very small.
Tiny wishes seem to hardly matter where they fall.
But small does not mean no one should hear the call.
A heart wish, even small, is important to us all.

Wishes
can be large and last a lifetime through.

And when there's years of waiting, make us feel blue.
But large wishes bring large rewards to you.
Then a large wish is worth the waiting for, too.

Wishes
can be for ourselves or for another,
Wishing for our friends, family, father, our mother.
Wishing hopes fulfilled for our sister, our brother.
Wishing for them is fulfilling like no other.

Wishes
for ourselves, they are important too,
But wishing for others comes full circle, is true.
So when you wish for others, wish wisely as you do.
What you wish for others will surely come to you.

Every wish
is really a soul's prayer.
Find a place and kneel, and wish your wish there.
God who hears all wishes answers where
The wisher humbly realizes
Every wish is really a prayer.

◆   ◆   ◆

And all things, whatsoever ye shall ask in prayer,
believing, ye shall receive.
Matthew 21:22

Ask and it shall be given unto you;
seek, and ye shall find;
knock, and it shall be opened unto you.
Matthew 7:7

◆   ◆   ◆

In I Peter 5:7, we are told to *cast all our cares upon* Jesus because he cares for us. Those *cares* are often worded by us as "wishes." I wish this…, or I wish that…, I wish I…, I wish they…and so on. Philippians 4:6 states *"in everything by prayer and supplication…let your requests be made known unto God."* Our requests can be translated in many cases as our wishes. Notice, it says: *in everything. Everything* includes well, everything—the big and the tiny, the very small. We often forget that a great big God is interested in our very tiny requests and wishes. But He is. However, we are also told that *"out of the same mouth proceedeth blessing and cursing…these things ought not to be so."* James 3:10 When we speak and pray, or wish for things for ourselves and others, choose blessing, not cursing. Do all things in love.

I Wish

I wish that I could see you one more time.
I wish these words had power
more than rhyme.
I wish that we could talk and laugh a while.
I wish that I could see
your beautiful smile.

But Heaven's road is marked
a one-way street,
And not until I too leave will we meet.
But still I find my heart
cry once again.
I'll battle truth and longing 'til the end.
The truth that loved one,
you will not come back.
And with longing, forward
I must go to fill my lack.

It seems that Heaven could let you get away.
Could you be missed
in eternity for a day?
But reason wrestles a battle with my heart.
Yes, yes, I knew the answer
from the start.

So, when I see you,
Dear one, in Heaven's eternity,
Oh run, oh run, straight,
Loved one, to me.
And smile the smile I've longed
so long to see,
And know that God fulfilled
a wish for me.

sorrow not even as others which have no hope

◆   ◆   ◆

*But I would not
have you to be ignorant, brethren,
concerning them which are asleep,
that ye sorrow not
even as others which have no hope.
For if we believe that Jesus died and rose again,
even so
them also which sleep in Jesus
will God bring with him.
I Thessalonians 4:13-14*

*I will ransom them
from the power of the grave;
I will redeem them from death:
O death, I will be thy plague;
O death, I will be thy destruction.
Hosea 13:14a*

*O death, where is
thy sting?
O grave, where is
thy victory?
I Corinthians 15:55*

◆   ◆   ◆

And so we look forward to the glorious day when we see our loved ones again, our loved ones that have died in Christ Jesus. In John 11:25 Jesus stated clearly why we are not like those without hope. Jesus said, *"I am the resurrection and the life: he that believeth in me, though he were dead, yet shall he live."* And our loved ones who sleep in Christ, who died before us, *yet shall they live.* And we will see that smile that we've longed so long to see and say too:

O, grave where is your victory?

them also which sleep in Jesus will God bring with him

Valley of the Shadow

Early morning
a new soft light begins to shimmer
Across spring green grass where a mother blue jay
Teaches her baby to fly amidst shadows that play.
Branches sway of the old willow. Move quicker.

Quicker,
Nudges the mother, as the baby slow
Lands by a tree, shadows of light glint on the blue
Of the determined mother, proud of her fledgling, too.
Wings flap and flutter to fly, stop then go.

Go.
And the children happy in the yard, run, run, run.
The light now grows strong to bright golden midday
Sun as the winds blow soft, shadows dance every way.
Dance every way as children play. Laughter and fun.

Fun and play
In the yard all day 'til the dinner hour's
Here, and Father with the hose walks and waters all around.
The sun in the west seems to be falling to the ground
As the shadows grow long on watered grass and flowers.

Flowers are picked
By children who come out for the end

Of evening sun and run to grandmother to give her one,
A pretty flower. She smiles and then the children run
Between shadows of the setting sun, and a kiss they send.

Send a kiss
As they wave good night. Only a little light
Remains amidst the valley of shadow everywhere.
Shadows cover the yard where children played without care
Amidst shadows all day, now sleeping safe in the night.

Night descends.
Walking through the last long shadow
As night falls where the shadows flickered all day.
I fear no evil, for Thou art with me all the way,
Though I walk through the valley of the shadow.

Shadow of death.
I will fear no evil.
For Thou art with me, and I with Thee.
Surely goodness and mercy follow me.
I will dwell in the house of the Lord forever.

◆   ◆   ◆

They that dwell
in the land of the shadow of death,
upon them hath the light shined.
Isaiah 9:2-7b

Yea, though I walk through
the valley of the shadow of death,
I will fear no evil, for thou art with me.
Psalm 23:4a

◆   ◆   ◆

Shadows are everywhere. Since the day of our birth, through all the years of our life, we have moved and walked and played and worked amidst shadows. They are everywhere, and they are harmless. And so is the *shadow of death* for those who are in Christ Jesus. How many times have many of us heard the twenty-third Psalm and John 3:16? Put them together and what do you have but the complete answer as to why the *shadow of death* is harmless, without sting. John 3:16 says: *For God so loved the world that He gave his only begotten son, that whosoever believeth in him should not perish, but have everlasting life.* Psalm 23: *I will fear no evil for thou art with me.* Who is with me that *I will fear no evil?* The *son,* Jesus, that died for me to have *everlasting life.*

Walking through the last long shadow
I fear no evil, for Thou art with me all the way,
Though I walk through the valley of the shadow.

Yea, though I walk through the valley of the shadow

And So We Say Goodbye

And so we say goodbye. Oh, goodbye. Goodbye.
We knew, we knew this time would come,
But I'm grieving this goodbye. I'm not the only one.
Please forgive me if I cry; hearing goodbye, I cry.

No, I'm not the only one grieving, missing you.
We rehearse the last words we each had to say.
We remember our last moments before today.
I'm not the only one missing you—so many do.

And we all knew our paths would someday part.
We know God plans, plans our lives that way
For a season—but today seemed not the day,
No, or the way. It seems too soon we are apart.

Too soon from our tiny, tiny point of view.
We struggle with the grand, majestic mystery.
Our lives intertwined have their own destiny.
To your heavenly view, oh God, our minds renew.

For a while we shared as travelers the road of life,
And we remember shared smiles and shared sorrow,
And hope shared, oh the hope shared for tomorrow.
And now your journey ends, set free from the strife.

We rejoice in your life, but tears roll down our face.
We let you go to the heavenly home that awaits you,
A home your brothers and sisters also long to go to.
As one of the runners, you finished well your race.

And so we say goodbye. Oh, goodbye. Goodbye.
Oh, I'm glad there is good in this difficult word,
Because the word now is so hard, hard to be heard.
But there is good in goodbye, even though we cry.

Joy will eclipse death's shadow and searing sorrow
Though our paths separate, it's for a short while.
In a tomorrow, face-to-face we'll meet and smile.
And we say goodbye, not forever, no, but for now.

So the final word is, as a tear rolls from our eye,
Is the word that makes us sad, brings us comfort too—
Goodbye means God be with ye, and God is with you,
And you are with God, and so we say goodbye.

◆   ◆   ◆

He will swallow up death
in victory;
and the Lord God
will wipe away tears from off all faces.
Isaiah 25:8

That whosoever believeth in Him
should not perish,
but
have eternal life. John 3:15

And this is the promise that he has promised us,
even eternal life. I John 2:25

◆   ◆   ◆

We say goodbye so many times during our lifetime—every day when
we leave our home, or work, or school—but when it is that "final"
goodbye, we usually experience varying levels of sadness.
However, we have God's promise, and what a magnificent promise it
is: *That whosoever believeth in Him…has eternal life.*
This is why Christ died that we might have life.
And so our confidence is, as the poem says:
"Though our paths separate, it's for a short while.
In a tomorrow, face-to-face we'll meet and smile."

this is the promise that he has promised us...eternal life

And So We Stand

◆

Remembering September 11th

And so we stand,
a great nation forged by God's almighty hand.
And so we stand,
every river flowing as God ordained and planned.
And so we stand,
with love and freedom our gift, extending to others a hand.
And so we stand,
a mighty people bound by love, a mighty band.
And so we stand,
every child, woman and man joining hand in hand.
And so we stand,
where there's fear and doubt, faith's light will help us understand.
And so we stand,
with the bright torch of freedom held high in our hand.
And so we stand,
when weapons are formed against us, united we'll take a stand.
And so we stand,
for those who fight for what is right, give them a hand.
And so we stand,
Army, Air Force, Navy, Marines, Coast Guard
defend liberty and land.

And so we stand,
the United States of America, pledging with heart and hand.
And so we stand,
God bless our land.

◆   ◆   ◆

And who is he that will harm you,
if ye be followers of that which is good?
I Peter 3:13

Therefore, brethren, stand fast and hold the traditions which ye have been
taught. II Thessalonians 2:15a

◆   ◆   ◆

stand fast and hold the traditions which ye have been taught

We Love Our Soldiers

We love our soldiers.
We love these brave, valiant women and men.
We stand by them, courageous warriors.
We love our soldiers and remember them.

Our country started with every-day patriots
Who were soldiers who fought the battle well.
They knew the price of freedom took guts.
So today our country rings loud the liberty bell.

We love our soldiers.
We love these brave, valiant women and men.
We stand by them, courageous warriors.
We love our soldiers and care for them.

We send our mighty soldiers our battles to fight,
Across the roaring oceans to vast lonely lands.
They fight through difficulties, the dark of night.
These brave soldiers know war's demands.

We love our soldiers.
We love these brave, valiant women and men.
We stand by them, courageous warriors.
We love our soldiers and hope for them.

We know the price is high for these brave souls,
But they know the price is higher if no one goes.
And so they lay their life down in dirty fox holes,
Or on a ship, a plane, or places only God knows.

We love our soldiers.
We love these brave, valiant women and men.
We stand by them, courageous warriors.
We love our soldiers and pray for them.

So bend your knee and look on high tonight.
God holds a special place for soldiers in heaven.
Our soldiers stand for freedom and what is right.
Soldiers risk life, the greatest gift that can be given.

We love our soldiers.
We love these brave, valiant women and men.
We stand by them, courageous warriors.
We love our soldiers. God bless our soldiers.

◆   ◆   ◆

Blessed be the Lord my strength, which teacheth my hands to war, and my fingers to fight: My goodness and my fortress;
my high tower and my deliverer; my shield and he in whom I trust.
Psalm 144: 1-2a

Through God we shall do valiantly:
for it is he that shall tread down our enemies. Psalms 60:12

He shall not be afraid of evil tidings:
his heart is fixed, trusting in the Lord.
Psalms 112:7

So that we may boldly say, The Lord is my helper, and
I will not fear what man shall do unto me. Hebrews 13:6

Be not afraid of sudden fear, neither of the desolation of the wicked, when
it cometh. For the Lord shall be thy confidence,
and shall keep thy foot from being taken. Proverbs 3:25-26

◆   ◆   ◆

God's word is filled with so many tremendous promises for ourselves
and for those we love. We admire, love and pray for those who serve
our country as soldiers. How wonderful to know our soldiers, and we
ourselves need not fear what man can do to us, when the *Lord is* our
helper and we are *trusting in* Him.

Friendship Through the Fire

Friendship through the fire.
Friendship through the rain.
Friendship through the joy.
Friendship through the pain.

The troubles are gentler.
The day is brighter.

Our path's crossing
was easy to explain.
God our meeting,
did ordain.

Friendship in the valley,
and walking the plain.
Friendship up the mountain
and down again.

The burdens are lighter.
The way is clearer.

Through our journey,
our gain

was our friendship
that God did ordain.

◆   ◆   ◆

For whom he did foreknow he did predestinate. Romans 8:29a

◆   ◆   ◆

The grand Master Planner did foresee our need and supplied us with a
special gift, *"for every good and perfect gift,"* as said in James, *"comes
down from the Father above."* The gift of friendship is forged stronger
and polished brighter
through the fire, our trials and the joys of our lives.

every good and perfect gift comes down from the Father

Guts and a Heart

✦

For those who Serve and Protect

The world is full of problems. People are a fallen race.
Many people are lost, needing direction.
Many people need mild to serious correction,
But people also need consideration and grace.
A police officer is made of two parts.
Both parts are important, neither part to neglect.
Both parts make an officer who will serve and protect.
To be a police officer it takes
Guts and a heart.

Guts is courage. Life gets rough.
Guts is facing difficult situations day after day.
Guts is standing up for the right way.
Guts is strong. Guts is tough.
Guts is half of the whole part—
Guts and a heart.

A heart knows people have worth that they serve.
A heart protects the innocent one every day.
A heart shows the wrong one the right way.
A heart is tough love. A heart takes nerve.

A heart is half of the whole part—
Guts and a heart.

The police officer sees the world of woe.
Serious offenses and small—
Police see it all.
Police see the world we know.
The problems of our world are not pretty.
Police face these problems in every city.

Where would we be if there weren't law officers,
Willing to serve and protect us all?
Law creates freedom to live in peace.

What would we do if there weren't men and women
Willing to answer the call?
Thank God for police.

Thank God for those who said yes and did answer
This worthy call;
They were willing to do their part.
Thank God for men and women police officers
All across this great land.
To be a police officer
It goes hand in hand—
It takes
Guts and a heart.

◆   ◆   ◆

And whosoever
will be chief among you
let him be your servant.
Even as the Son of man
came not to be ministered unto,
but to minister;
and to give his life
a ransom for many.
Matthew 20:27-28

◆   ◆   ◆

Jesus has told us to serve.
He has even said
that they who are willing to serve are *chief among* us.
With the many difficulties that must be dealt with daily in a fallen
world, we need to be grateful for those who are willing to *serve* and
protect us. Be thankful for those who serve you, and take up your cross
too. Serving others is a calling for all Christians.
That is what Christ did: he came to serve, not to be served. And we are
to be like him. Think—how can I serve someone today?

A Fireman's Daughter

Well, I'm a fireman's daughter.
I'm proud of that; it's true.
My daddy put out fires
And saved many lives too.

I remember one Christmas day,
I asked my mom, putting presents by the tree,
"We're celebrating our Savior's birth today.
Why does Daddy have to be away from me?"
My mama looked me in the eyes and said,
"He's laying down his life for others to be saved.
Daddy's doing what our Savior did."

Well, I'm a fireman's daughter.
I'm proud of that; it's true.
My daddy put out fires
And saved many lives too.

One time at church a man spoke to me
About firemen in a passing way.
"It seems they sit around; that's what I see.
What do firemen do all day?"
My Sunday school teacher smiling said, "I'll tell.
Yes, they wait, but when they hear the fire bell,
To save lives, they run straight into hell."

Well, I'm a fireman's daughter.
I'm proud of that; it's true.
My daddy put out fires
And saved many lives too.

Senior prom night, Mama said to me,
"This is something Daddy won't want to miss."
She drove me to the firehouse for Daddy to see.
Mama took a picture. Daddy gave me a kiss.
And my dad said, wearing his uniform of blue,
"Honey, you're beautiful. I'm so proud of you."
We waved goodbye, proud of my father too.

Well, I'm a fireman's daughter.
I'm proud of that; it's true.
My daddy put out fires
And saved many lives too.

On 9-11 many brave firefighters died.
Into burning buildings they went, others to save.
For those who sacrificed their lives, I cried,
And for their families standing at a grave.
This fireman's daughter said, "For firemen I pray.
Greater love has no man than to give his life that way.
America's proud of its heroes who died that day."

Well, I'm a fireman's daughter.
I'm proud of that; it's true.
My daddy put out fires
And saved many lives too.

◆   ◆   ◆

Greater love hath no man than this, that a man
lay down his life for his friends. John 15:13

◆   ◆   ◆

The Bible is filled with the stories of many heroes: David against Goli-
ath, Daniel in the lion's den, and the many men and women followers
of Christ who were willing to be persecuted for their faith as spoken of
in Hebrews, chapter eleven. There are still today those in the world
who are persecuted for their faith in Christ. They are heroes for the
faith. And yet heroes exist in our everyday life. On September 11, 9-
11, we saw these everyday heroes come out of the woodwork, and *lay
down* their lives for their fellow men. Jesus said there is no greater love
than this.

Greater love hath no man than this, that a man lay down his life

My Mom Said

"It's just the angels bowling," my mom said,
As thunder crashed with lightning overhead.
Perhaps my mother didn't always have her doctrine right,
But I slept peacefully on my pillow that night.
"A dandelion under your chin, yellow shows if you like butter."
Perhaps my mom wasn't always a very scientific mother,
But still in summer I hold a dandelion under my chin,
Like Mom did; that's where the tradition did begin.

"Don't make that funny face," Mom said to us at the dinner table.
"Your face could freeze that way, and you'll never be able
To change it. Wear clean under clothes just in case some day
You're in an accident, and they have to carry you away."
Perhaps my mother made her points in a strange way,
But I still remember the lessons 'til today.
Perhaps my mom wasn't always doctrinally correct,
But the most important lessons of life, she didn't neglect.

What I remember most about mother was this:
She sealed each evening with a bedtime kiss.
She lived the golden rule and wanted people to be treated fair.
And she taught her children to say a bedtime prayer.
And Mom said funny things about salt and silverware,
That company would come if we dropped it here and there.

"Knock on wood," for this and that, she'd smile and say.
She'd hold out a wishbone, "Make a wish today."

Perhaps my mother even herself she would amuse.
But I know the most important lessons she didn't confuse.
Perhaps my mom wasn't always doctrinally perfect,
But the most important lessons of life, she didn't neglect.
There were many other things that were rather odd,
But most important, my mom said, "Love people, and love God."

◆   ◆   ◆

Love the Lord thy God and...love thy neighbor. Mark 12:30a-31b

Love the Lord...love thy neighbor

When Grandma Put Her China Out

When Grandma put her china out, we started with a prayer.
Together we would bow our heads around the table there.
Bless us, oh Lord, and these thy gifts we are about to receive.
When Grandma put her china out,
It was a wonderful occasion, a holiday.
When Grandma put her china out,
The dinner was special for everyone, in every way.
The china was so beautiful and the glasses of water
Seemed to sparkle. Conversation was light,
but it all seemed to matter.
The tablecloth was linen. It was starched and shiny,
And the flowers along the edge were Grandma's embroidery.
Grandma's home-baked rolls were passed around
in a basket of wood,
And nothing in your life ever seemed to smell so fresh and good.
After rolls, the vegetables went from hand to hand;
that included peas.
And today my brothers and I would eat everything and say, please,
And thank you, or Dad would certainly give us the look,
But today we all wanted to do everything by the book.
Because when Grandma put her china out
It was a wonderful occasion,

And everyone wanted to be at his very best
For this feast, a family celebration.
From Thy bounty through Christ, our Lord.
We had cranberries, luscious stuffing,
gravy and potatoes mashed just right,
And the turkey drew awe when it was in everyone's sight.
Grandpa had his job, and he took his time
carving the turkey just so;
Dad helped him out and my brothers watched in a row.
We were told children were starving somewhere,
and it seemed so sad,
But today it was easy to eat everything on our plate that we had.
I'm sure there were other problems in the world that day.
And I imagine there were other tribulations
that Mother and Father didn't say,
And Grandmother and Grandfather had health concerns
and bills to pay.
But when Grandma put her china out,
For a while the world was perfect in every way.
When Grandma put her china out,
joy and hope filled the house, not gloom.
Next came dessert, and for the moment our greatest worry was,
Is there room?
And Mother asked Grandmother, "How did you make this?"
And she said:
Butter and a dash of this, and a some of that.
All of the recipe was in her head.
The smell of fresh apple and pumpkin pie
was a moment we waited for.

Grandma told how she cut and cored apples
Grandpa bought at a corner store.
And even washing the beautiful china dishes didn't seem a chore.
Because you wanted this day to last and last
and go on forever more.
Because when Grandmother put her china out,
It was a memorable time from the start.
But now when Grandma puts her china out,
It's only a memory in my heart.
I remember when Grandma put her china out,
we started with a prayer when
Together as a family we bowed our heads together there and said,
Amen.

◆   ◆   ◆

It was meet that we should make merry and be glad.
Luke 15:32a

◆   ◆   ◆

It is meet; it is right that we should have times to feast and celebrate. It makes our bonds with our family and friends stronger. It also shows our gratefulness to God for all that we do have, even when there are other problems going on in the world and in our lives. It is right that we take time to be *merry* and *be glad*.

A Bed of Roses

Life is a bed of roses on this earth, life is each day.
And along with all the beautiful roses
come the thorns that get in the way.
Who told you life's a bed of roses? Well, they were right.
Life is a fragrant beautiful bed of roses,
but life can change over night.
Soft petals of pink, gold and red roses
Fall in the mud, stepped on, a sad sight.
Life truly is a bed of roses,
A colorful array, a sensuous, rich treasure,
But all the beauty of all the roses
Stays only for a time, a short measure.
And when touching bushes of roses
We must handle them with care.
We draw near to the lovely roses,
But along with the roses, there's a snare.
Hidden there—the thorn of the roses
Amidst the beauty—there is pain.
But our lives, like the roses,
Without embracing would be no gain.
If we never desired in our lives roses
Because of the thorn's pain,
We'd miss God's gift of roses
Like wanting sunshine, never rain.

But we need rain to bring the roses,
So this is a riddle life gives,
Answered by the bed of roses;
All must embrace this truth as one lives.
Life is a fragrant, glorious bed of roses.
Life is, even in the every-day mundane.
And along with all the glorious roses
Come thorns that will bring pain.
Life on this earth is a bed of roses
With thorns—until we leave someday.
Then all that will be left is the glorious roses.
Gone will be the pain that came our way.
Life is a gift, a gift of beautiful roses,
Yet there are painful thorns within it too.
When embracing life's roses,
Feeling the painful piercing of the thorn,
Walk with the One among the roses
Who a King's crown of thorns has worn.
Life is a bed of beautiful roses.
Life is a bed of roses with the thorn's pain.
Life is a bed of roses.
To understand this truth is great gain.

◆   ◆   ◆

Then came Jesus forth, wearing the crown of thorns.
John 19:5a

These things have I spoken unto you
that in me ye might have peace.
In the world ye shall have tribulation:
but be of good cheer; I have overcome the world.
John 16:33

◆   ◆   ◆

A favorite old hymn says,
"I come to the garden alone
while the dew is still on the roses."
And what is found there amidst the roses?
There "He walks with me
and He talks with me."
And to add to the preciousness
of this place
there "He tells me, 'I am his own.'"
And the hymn writer goes on to say,
as they "tarry *there*" together
amidst the bed of roses, *there* is joy.
Yes, *there* together is joy and peace.

*These things have I spoken unto you
that in me ye might have peace.*

If the Heart

If the heart
lives without music,
it sighs.
If the heart
lives without poetry,
it cries.
If the heart
lives without love,
it dies.

So let us
share music
together and sing.
So let us
to others
beautiful words bring.
So let us
give love,
the most important thing.

◆   ◆   ◆

Praise the Lord.
Sing unto the Lord a new song,
and his praise in the congregation of saints. Proverbs 149:1

Heaviness in the heart of man maketh it stoop:
but a good word maketh it glad. Proverbs 12:25

A new commandment I give unto you That ye love one another;
as I have loved you, that ye also love one another.
By this shall all men know that ye are my disciples,
if ye have love one to another. John 13: 34, 35

◆   ◆   ◆

Never think you have nothing to give. A song to share, a kind word, a simple expression of love is much to give to another.

If God

If God could wear a face,
I'd see Him in this place.
He'd share smiles, laughter and tears
With loving arms and listening ears.
God's caring is here and written
On the faces of those I see
Who share this home with me.

If God could show me love,
And not be distant or far above;
If God could be so real that
I'd see Him every day,
Then living here has been that way.

If God is someone who loves us
Just as we are,
And knows us for who we are,
Gives us love that will stay
Beyond our easy todays,
Into our hard tomorrows,
Holds us through our sorrows,
Understands our broken dreams to mend,
And gives us hope to believe and dream again.

If God is real
And His word is true;
If God promises to never leave us
And be with us in all we do.
If God loves and laughs
And cares and gives,
Then living here proves God lives
And loves His children as we are,
And never really is too far away to care.

If two thousand years ago,
Christ left this earth
But said He'd always with us be,
Then a great miracle is here to see.
That Christ, who once walked Galilee,
Died on the cross for you and me,
Rose into Heaven's eternity,
Now walks and talks
And lives and loves
In this home through you and me.

If God could wear a face,
I'd see Him in this place.

◆　　◆　　◆

I will never leave thee,
nor forsake thee.
Hebrews 13: 5b

And I will pray the Father,
and he shall give you
another Comforter,
that he may abide with you
forever even the Spirit of truth;
whom the world cannot receive,
because it seeth him not,
neither knoweth him:
but ye know him
for he dwelleth with you,
and shall be in you.
John 14: 16, 17

◆   ◆   ◆

Shouldn't others be able to say, they see Christ in you?
If the Spirit *dwelleth with you* and *in you*,
should not your face, hands, heart be a reflection of Him?

Tears Become Flowers

Sitting alone on a wooden park bench,
sitting in the lonely place,
I thought no one had noticed a silent tear slipping down my face.
As I wiped the tear across my cheek, an old woman sat by me.
"Do you know the way?" she said. I looked at her and could see
She was talking to and smiling at me. Her old face
had the lines of life.
She sat with her hands folded as if to pray; her hair sparkled white.
"Pardon me," I said. "Do you know the way?" she repeated.
I wondered, was she lost? And before my
thought was completed,
"Do you know the way," she inquired,
"to make tears become flowers?"
I looked at her inquisitively; I wondered, did I hear her right?
I had sat alone for hours.
I squinted at her; the afternoon sun shone behind her.
I wondered what to do,
And what did she mean? She, too, was alone.
Perhaps I could give her a minute or two.
As if she knew what I had thought, she then continued
"Don't catch the tear.
It's simple. To make a tear turn into a flower,
don't catch the tear, my dear,

Let it fall, fall to the ground." She looked into my eyes,
smiling sweetly still.
"Just let the tears fall and the tears will become rain,
and the rain will
Water seeds of flowers, flowers of hope.
They're buried in the ground."
She sighed a deep sigh, looked into the sky.
"Seeds of hope flowers are all around."
Now she motioned with her hands around the park.
"Hope flowers grow from those
Who take their tears of pain and turn them into rain.
Their tears are especially chosen.
For a special seed, more special than any other.
These are watered only by tears of pain.
That's been turned into rain."
Her hand touched mine as she continued to explain.
Glorious rain. Rain. Rain. Rain.
It's been dry lately. Oh, there is such a great need."
Again she said, with a soft sigh,
"There is such a need to water this seed.
But only those who take their pain
and turn it into rain can water this
Special seed." Now I sighed too. Was this an opportunity
I wouldn't want to miss?
I looked at her again. She had the hands
of a gentle gardener. And my,
How she talked of seeds, flowers and rain.

I will pray the Father, and he shall give you
another Comforter, that he may abide with you forever

But, she also talked of hope and pain. Why?

Could I help this dear old woman,

who made me forget my own pain? Even

If it wasn't completely gone, being near her, wanting to help, seemed
to make it lessen

Just the same. Could I help with this need?

She had the smile of a sweet old

Grandma "I'll help!" I said, suddenly shouting out,

feeling, strong and bold.

"Oh," she said, "I'm so glad, Dear." I felt surprised,

but she looked like she always knew.

I said, "But what do I do?"

"When I come back tomorrow you'll know what to do."

She patted my hand and I felt such warmth and peace.

"For a little longer, can you stay?"

She said, "I must go," with a smile that said,

please understand, she walked away.

"Tomorrow around two?" I said.

She looked into my eyes, smiled and nodded her head.

As I sat on the bench to wait the following day,

I thought of all the words she said.

How tears become flowers. At two-o-clock

a child walked up, handing me a flyer.

"Thank you," I said, as I patiently waited for my new grandmotherly
friend to appear.

Time passed. I checked my watch every hour. It was six.

People went home for dinner.

Then a young woman strolled by me and noticed

my hand still holding the paper.

She looked at me and said, "Did you give that any thought? Holding
back my tears,
I questioned, "What do you mean?"
"The flyer the kids passed out, we need volunteers
To supervise one day a week the children from the orphanage
who play here at the park.
The need is so great." As she walked away,
I let my tears fall to the ground in the dark.
That was years ago and I still come back to this park bench.
I love to see everywhere
All the beautiful flowers blooming, and I think of
the special children I took care
Of and the ones I met in hospitals too,
and the nursing homes I now visit.
Oh, and all soldiers I wrote and corresponded with,
and that's not even all of it.
So many places I did volunteer my time,
and with others I would share
The simple gifts God had given me and mainly, it seems,
I just took time to care.
But as I sit here on this bench, I still find myself hoping
that I'll some day see
With all these lovely flowers, the dear old woman
who once sat on this bench with me.
As I mused about the things she said so long ago,
I noticed a man sitting alone
On the bench next to me. He took his hand and wiped
a tear across his face. In a soft tone
I said, as I walked toward him and sat down on the bench,

consider one another to provoke unto love and good works

"Do you know the way?"
I continued to inquire, "to make tears become flowers?"
He looked at me and as I
Folded my hands together, he said, "I'm not sure I understand why
You have asked me that question, but I notice
that you have the hands of a gardener."
He looked and squinted, the sun setting behind me,
"And you have a grandmother
Face, a kindly, grandmother face," he said,
looking at my hair so white, "Please explain."
I continued, "Don't catch the tears;
let the tears fall and the tears will become rain,
And the rain will water seeds of flowers of hope.
They're buried in the ground." And
As I talked about the need he surprised himself, but not me,
saying, "I'd like to lend
A hand to help, but what can I do?"
He said sighing, looking down at his feet.
And I said with a grin, I'll explain to you tomorrow
at two-o-clock here we'll meet.
And as I slowly shuffled off, he asked
if I could just a little longer stay.
I turned and smiled, waved goodbye,
and I knew he understood I had to be on my way.

◆   ◆   ◆

And let us consider one another
to provoke unto love and good works. Hebrews 10:24

And we know that all things work together for good
to them that love God. Romans 8:28

Let brotherly love continue.
Be not forgetful to entertain strangers: for thereby
some have entertained angels unawares. Hebrews 13:1-2

◆   ◆   ◆

Not all things are good, but God can work *all things together for good.*
In the word volunteers, you hear the word, the homonym, "tears." A
lesson exists in the word. That which is sad, difficult, or painful may
not be good, but can work out *for good.*

Goodbye, Hello

✦

Go, Graduate. Go, go!

An ending, but an exhilarating beginning.
Something stopped, but you're off and running.
And once again you're wondering,
What will you be doing?

One door closes, one opens world-wide.
A small world behind you, a giant world outside.
Mostly you're cheerfully laughing, but inside
A tender tear you cried.

Firm faith, but you're unsure.
Knowing, but still unclear.
Holding on to hope, love, letting go of fear
In this wondrous new year.

Daring to dream. A future before, a past behind.
Some things to forget, some things to remind.
What will be lost? What will you find?
Keeping both in mind.

Hearts hold on as hands let go.
Feet move with certainty to a future you don't know,

But you're hearing in your ear: yes, go slow,
Or a definite no!

Goodbye, hello in the same breath.
The old season ends. A season joyously gives birth.
You see life's short; you see its awe-inspiring width,
Its infinite depth.

Exit, friends, who were like family, teachers,
Enter, family-like friends and mentors.
Heaven with the earth wildly cheers.
Loved ones clapping in the bleachers.
Go, graduate. Go, go!

◆   ◆   ◆

Rejoice with them that
do rejoice.
Romans 12:15a

But let the righteous
be glad;
let them rejoice
before God; yea,
let them exceedingly rejoice.
Psalm 68:3

And thine ear
shall hear a word behind thee,
saying,

This is the way, walk ye in it
when ye turn
to the right hand, and to the left.
Isaiah 30:21

The steps
of a good man
are ordered by the Lord
and he delighteth
in his way.
Psalms 37:23

◆　　　◆　　　◆

Every beginning is an ending.
Every ending is a beginning;
and the *just shall walk by their faith.*

This is the way, walk ye in it

Racer, Dream Chaser

Racer, dream chaser.
Power behind the wheel. Moving metal and steel.
Turning rubber. Burning rubber.
Storms of dust. Furious noise. Racing—a sport not for boys.
But boys and girls watch these men with their powerful toys.
A sound of whirring, then a blurring.
Cars rolling with thunder, moving as a flash of light.
Like men of ancient lore, drivers wear the helmet of a knight,
A racer, a dream chaser.
Danger at the turn.
Those who aren't ready will learn.
This is a sport where men are men,
But sometimes a daring woman competes with them.
Seconds count, every hour. Pushing the pedal for power.
Speeding with the risk of the crash.
Making an accelerated, exhilarating dash,
At the sight of the waving checkered flag.
Not wishing just to brag,
But to conquer, to race against defeat,
The inner challenges to meet
In the race that all face—the challenge to win
The race they did begin.
Lap after lap, now the finish line is clear.
Winning the race is near and dear.

Not looking back since the challenge began.
Racing for the victory, to finish the race they've run.
Crowds roar with the engine of the racer,
Cheering the dream chaser.
Achieving the dream they did chase,
Crossing the finish line, finishing well the race.
The thrill of being alive. The victory lap to drive.
Winning—to be victorious. It is grand. It is glorious.
Racer, dream chaser.

◆   ◆   ◆

Know ye not
that they which run in a race run all,
but one
receives the prize?
So run, that ye may obtain.
I Corinthians 9:24

Wherefore seeing we also are compassed about
with so great a cloud of witnesses,
let us lay aside every weight,
and the sin which doth so easily beset us,
and let us run with patience
the race
that is set before us, Looking unto Jesus-
the author and finisher of our faith;
who for the joy set before him endured

the cross,
despising the shame,
and is set down now
at the right hand of the throne of God.
Hebrews 12:1-2

◆　　　◆　　　◆

God's word says we are all in a *race*. There is a *race set before us*. And we are being watched just like those who race in a car race or at a track meet, or in another racing competition. And we need to do things to be successful in this race just as a wise competitor knows. We must *lay aside* the things which weigh us down, *the sin* that drags us down. We also need *patience* to run well the race, and we need to be *looking unto Jesus*. Remember he too had a race *set before* him—the cross.—He ran successfully to the finish line, when on the cross he said: *It is finished*.—But how did he finish well? By looking at the *joy set before him*. We have joy set before us, too. Let's run our race that we may hear God say to us:
Well done, thou good and faithful servant. Matthew 25:21a

Never Give Up

Never give up the ship that sails.
Never leave 'lone the babe that wails.
Search o'er for the mountain
that touches the sky.
Never give up. Never say die.

When seas are rough sailing, they are a discouragement.
When things are new, they cry for nourishment.
Mountains are everywhere,
to climb takes encouragement.
Never give up.

If a dream is worth pursuing,
If a goal is worthy of doing,
Never give up. Don't let it die.

Winds change. They'll blow a new way,
and the ship's sails will take flight.
Babies change. They'll grow,
and their crying will end one night.
But mountains will stay. They are everywhere.
So search for the mountain with the highest stair.
Search for the mountain that touches the sky.
Never give up. Never say die.
Never give up.

◆　　◆　　◆

*And let us not be weary in well-doing: for in due season we shall reap, **if** we faint not. Galatians 6:9*

◆　　◆　　◆

Is the dream worth pursuing? Is it worthy of doing?
If yes, then no—never give up!

for in due season we shall reap

One More Word

One more word
out of you
And I'll have to ask you
for two.
Then, three words,
and even four,
Five and six words,
and some more.
Seven, eight words,
nine and ten.
One more word,
we'll do it again.

One more word
out of you
And I'll have to ask you
for a few.
Maybe two words,
three and four,
Five and six words,
and much more.
Seven, eight words,
nine and ten.

One more word,
no two—the end.

But,
One more word
out of you
And I'll have to ask you…

◆   ◆   ◆

How beautiful on the mountain are the feet of those
who bring good news. Romans 10:15

◆   ◆   ◆

And good news, good words, are worth repeating again and again.

0-595-66010-X

Printed in the United States
21314LVS00001BC/10-12